PARENTING IS WONDER-FULL

SUE MILLER AND HOLLY DELICH

PARENTING IS WONDER-FULL

Published by Orange
a division of The reThink Group, Inc.
5870 Charlotte Lane, Suite 300
Cumming, GA 30040 U.S.A.

All Scripture quotations, unless otherwise noted, are taken from the Holy Bible, New International Version®. NIV®. Copyright © 1973, 1978, 1984 by International Bible Society. Used by permission of Zondervan.

Other Orange products are available online and direct from the publisher. Visit our website at www.ThinkOrange.com for more resources like these.

ISBN: 978-1-63570-000-8

Writers: Sue Miller, Holly Delich
Editorial Team: Karen Wilson, Kristen Ivy
Art Direction: Ryan Boon
Design: Industry Communications, j gribble
doodles and drawings, j gribble & killian gribble
Photographer: Sarah Joiner

Printed in the United States of America
Second Edition 2014

4 5 6 7 8 9 10 11 12 13

04/03/2017

ISN'T PARENTING WONDER-FULL?

AND ALSO A LITTLE . . .

★ TERRIFYING,
★ EXHAUSTING,
★ EXHILARATING,
★ MESSY,
★ LOVELY,
★ OVERWHELMING,
★ AMAZING,
★ CONFUSING,
★ AWESOME,
★ ALL CONSUMING,
★ ADVIL-INDUCING?

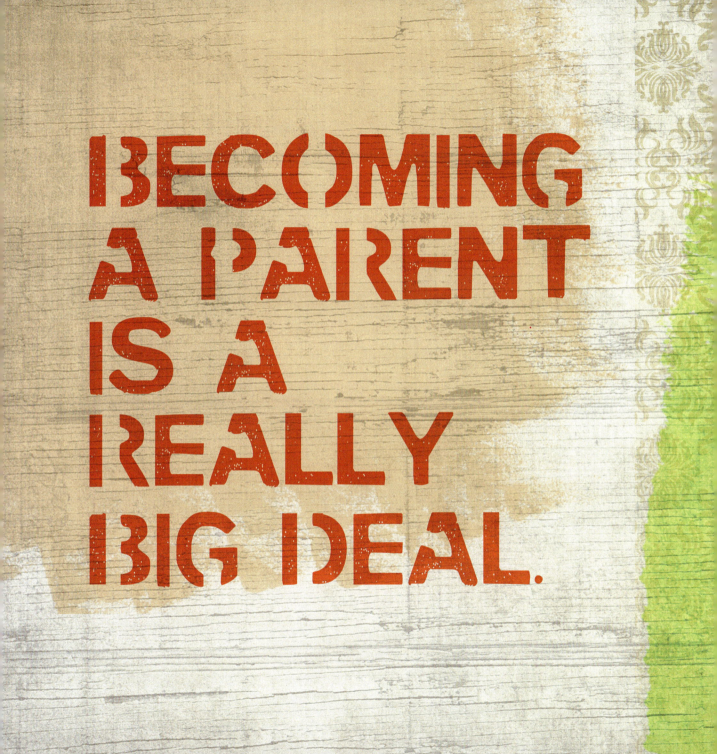

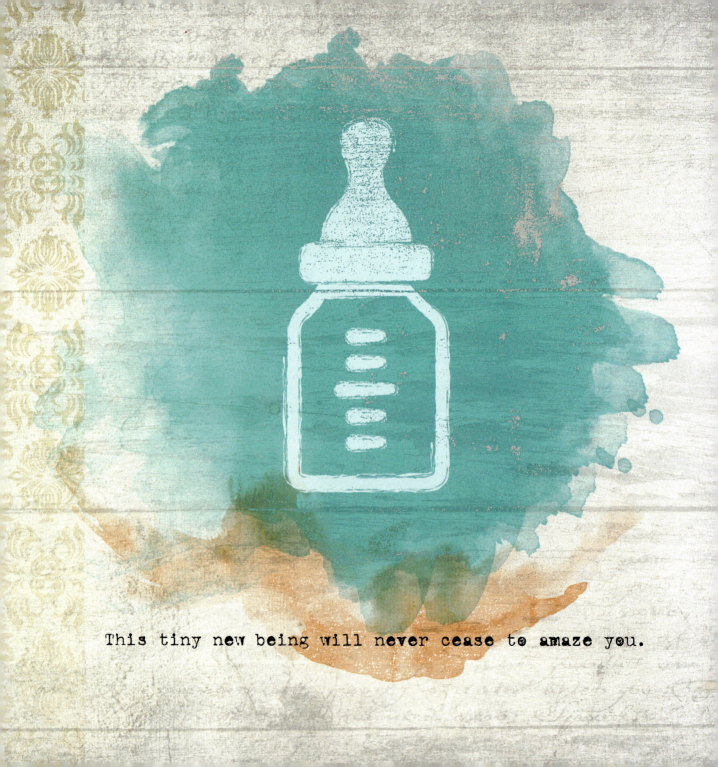

This tiny new being will never cease to amaze you.

BABY FACTS

- A baby's brain will double in the first year to become half of its overall size.

- Babies are born with 300 bones. Adults have 206.

- Babies can recognize their mother at birth by her voice and smell.

- Newborns can hear as well as you.

- Babies can see 8 to 15 inches away—the perfect distance to be able to see the face of whoever is feeding them.

- Babies born in May are the heaviest on average.

- Touch is one of baby's most advanced senses at birth.

- Babies have no tears until week three.

No matter how you got your little person, or what situation you find yourself in . . .

WHEN THIS HAPPENS TO YOU, YOU MAY BEGIN TO WONDER THINGS YOU NEVER DID

BEFORE.

YOU MAY WONDER...

WHAT HAVE I GOTTEN MYSELF INTO?

You have gotten yourself
into a **RELATIONSHIP**.

WE ALL START OUT WITH A PICTURE OF WHAT WE THINK FAMILY SHOULD LOOK LIKE.

Then we actually have a family.
And we discover it's not exactly
like we thought it would be.

WHAT SURPRISED YOU THE MOST ABOUT BECOMING A PARENT?

"I never knew how much I would loathe my dog. One time, he woke the baby barking at the UPS guy and I almost packed his puppy suitcase. #SchnauzerForSale"

"I could stare at her all day long. I miss her when she's sleeping. #Obsessed"

"I would pay someone a trillion dollars to get my baby to sleep right now. #WillingToStealIt #TheyLetYouSleepInJail"

"The grossest things don't even faze us. My husband uses that nose-suctioning thing, literally sucking the snot out of our baby daughter, and we don't even blink. #ClearEyesClearNoseCantLose"

"Every day ends with the same dilemma: What do I want more: sleep, food or a shower? #AlwaysSleep #DryShampoo"

"I am paranoid about every little thing. I never thought I'd be a helicopter parent, but I see germs everywhere. #IUseHandSanitizerLikeABoss"

THE POINT IS PARENTING IS COMPLICATED.

You constantly feel like a rookie playing in the World Series and the stakes are immeasurably high. Once you think you have it figured out, the game changes. But there are no do overs, no trial runs. You only get one chance to parent this child, and you don't want to mess up.

That's a lot of pressure. Maybe this job should have come with a ten-page application□references needed. . . or at least an instruction manual.

There really is no book on how to do this. No ONE perfect way.

SOME PEOPLE WILL GIVE YOU CRAZY ADVICE LIKE THIS.

Eden Hayes @edenhayes123   28 min
I've heard SIDS can be caused by stuffed animals.

Edde Campbell @Edde26   29 min
Crib bumpers can cause SIDS. #DontUseEm

David Candler @daveyc3po   38 min
SIDS? What is that?!?!

Sandra Everleigh @sanever   38 min
If your child sleeps in another room it can cause SIDS!

Eden Hayes @edenhayes123   45 min
@carol8316 Organic diapers are far better for the environment.

Sara McNally @nallyMC   58 min
@carol8316 Disposable diapers are the way to go! #ThrowAway

Elizabeth Carol @carol8316   38 min
Use cloth diapers, it's not that much of a hassle.

Sara McNally @nallyMC   1 hr
Make sure they have tummy time.

Jimmy O'Dell @dudeurgettinodell
Don't ever let them sleep on their tummy.

Eden Hayes @edenhayes123   2 hrs
Co-sleeping is the only way to get them to sleep.

Sandra Everleigh @sanever   2 hrs
Never let them nap in the car. Don't ever co-sleep.

Neve Darnell @neved8   2 hrs
Let them create their own schedule.

Edde Campbell @Edde26   3 hrs
Putting your kids on a schedule is so important. Remember, it's #EatPlaySleep

Christina Jankins @CJWWing   2 min
@sanever Don't go to the ER, they'll catch something else. #GermInfested

Neve Darnell @neved8   4 min
@sanever It's thrush.

Elizabeth Carol @carol8316   10 min
@sanever It's chicken pox.

Edde Campbell @Edde26   14 min
@sanever It's teething.

Jimmy O'Dell @dudeurgettinodell   16 min
@sanever It's just gas.

Eden Hayes @edenhayes123   18 min
@sanever It's reflux.

Sandra Everleigh @sanever   25 min
Baby's not sleeping. I think it's colic.

Neve Darnell @neved8   28 min
WE DON'T KNOW WHAT CAUSES SIDS!

Eden Hayes @edenhayes123   28 min
I've heard SIDS can be caused by stuffed animals.

Edde Campbell @Edde26   29 min
Crib bumpers can cause SIDS. #DontUseEm

David Candler @daveyc3po   38 min
SIDS? What is that?!?!

Sandra Everleigh @sanever   38 min
If your child sleeps in another room it can cause SIDS!

Eden Hayes @edenhayes123   45 min
@carol8316 Organic diapers are far better for the environment.

Sara McNally @nallyMC   58 min
@carol8316 Disposable diapers are the way to go! #ThrowAway

Elizabeth Carol @carol8316   38 min
Use cloth diapers, it's not that much of a hassle.

Sara McNally @nallyMC   1 hr
Make sure they have tummy time.

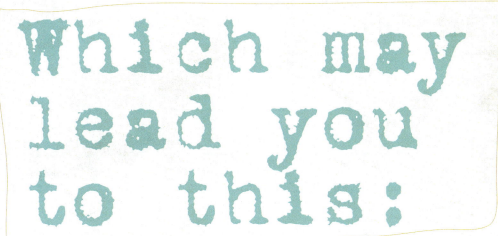

Which may lead you to this:

milkshakes - putting your pediatrician on speed dial - self-doubt - uncontrollable sobbing - anxiety medication - middle-of-the-night calls to your mother - arguing - confusion - late night reality TV - Oreo cookies

BUT TAKE HEART ...

These kids turned out fine, and so will yours!

This is Jessie. She nursed till she was three. She is now a marine biologist.

This is Peyton. She lived on Cheetos® and Flintstone® vitamins. She graduated Suma Cum Laude.

This is Steven. He slept on his parents' floor until he was nine. He doesn't do that anymore.

This is Rocky. The only way he would use the potty is backwards so he could play army men on the tank. He is now married with kids of his own.

This is Lee. He bit everyone in preschool. He is now a very kind pediatrician.

This is Mya. During preschool testing, she identified all numbers as the letter "P." Now, she's a 4th grade teacher.

OF COURSE, YOU WILL MAKE MISTAKES AS A PARENT TOO.

YOU MIGHT. . .

- bribe them with candy to get them into the car faster.
- forget that it's pajama day at school.
- settle for McDonald's ten days in a row.
- let them hold on to their Wubby longer than they should.
- lose track of them for a minute too long.

But that's okay! It really is. Say this out loud and embrace the imperfection: "My child is not perfect, and neither am I!"

It's okay because you're not in this for an Instagram-able life.

SO, BACK TO THE QUESTION:
WHAT HAVE
YOU GOTTEN
YOURSELF INTO?

A RELATIONSHIP.

YOUR RELATIONSHIP WITH YOUR CHILD IS MORE IMPORTANT THAN GETTING EVERYTHING RIGHT.

So, loosen up a little. Be easier on yourself.
Let go of whatever image you're trying to protect.

Maybe you should stress less and

play more,
cuddle more,
laugh more . . .

Just remember:

Kids get messy, and so does family.

Kids don't need perfect parents to turn out great.
What they do need is for you to invest in your
relationship with them.

This will take time. Years, in fact. But the good
news is time is on your side right now, and you're
off to a great start! You haven't even made any MANY
mistakes yet.

YOU MAY WONDER...

DID I DO ANYTHING THIS WEEK THAT REALLY MATTERS?

Yes, being present **matters.**

TODAY'S PERSONAL GOALS:

- ★ Shower
- ★ Write a bestselling book
- ★ Climb Mount Kilimanjaro
- ★ Learn Chinese
- ★ Run a half marathon
- ★ Cook a 7-course dinner

TODAY'S ACTUAL ACCOMPLISHMENTS:

Kept one tiny human alive, clothed, fed, changed, rested and entertained.

game **set** match

PARENTING IS NOT THE FLASHIEST OF GIGS. IT'S MADE UP OF HUNDREDS OF SMALL, REPETITIVE TASKS.

Nobody claps when you change nine newborn diapers a day or finally convince them to try the baby peas.

Surprisingly, there are no awards for the stamina it takes to hold a baby and make dinner one-handed.

There's no ribbon for the patience you showcase when asked to "Watch this!" "Watch this! Watch this!" no less than four billion times a day.

But it doesn't mean you don't deserve one.

So many hours of our time as parents are filled with mundane tasks that do not seem extraordinary or remarkable in any way. The list feels endless.

DID YOU KNOW THAT
EVERY PARENT HAS
APPROXIMATELY 936 WEEKS
TO SPEND WITH THEIR
CHILD FROM BIRTH TO
HIGH SCHOOL GRADUATION?

Imagine those 936 weeks as marbles in a jar, and with each week that goes by, you take a marble out.

Do the math. Based on your baby's age, how many marbles do you have left in your jar? _____

(There's actually a free app to help you keep track: the Legacy Countdown App.)

Can you believe you've already lost some marbles?

The jar of marbles illustrates an important principle: When you see how much time you have left, you tend to do more with the time you have now.

NOW, YOU MAY BE THINKING AS A PARENT:

"That's a really stupid idea. I already feel enough pressure. Besides, they're only five days . . . five weeks . . . or five months old! I can't wait to be reminded every day that I am running out of time with my kids."

But here's the really good news! You will never have more time to influence them than you do now.

That's why what you do this week matters. These first years, the ones with the 24-hour shifts, are the foundation builders for your relationship with your child. This week, you demonstrated that you are:

Dependable.
Trustwothy.
Safe.

Every time you showed up in the middle of the night, you made your marble count. Every time you read Goodnight, Moon or sang "Five Little Monkeys" for the umpteenth time, you made your marble count.

You are creating history together with your newest family member.

Now, maybe you're home with your child, all day long, or you're working a full-time job at the same time. Maybe you have help, or you're doing this all alone. . .

So, understand this: You don't have to make the most of every minute of every day. It's what you are doing consistently over a collection of days and weeks that will make a difference.

SO, BACK TO THE QUESTION:
DID YOU DO ANYTHING THAT REALLY MATTERS THIS WEEK?

YES.

BECAUSE SOMETIMES BEING DEPENDABLE IS MORE IMPORTANT THAN DOING SOMETHING REMARKABLE.

Being present IS one of the most remarkable things you can do at this stage in your child's life.

Don't forget, most people who are making history don't even know it.

Over the next 936 weeks, (935, 934, 933 . . .) you are creating history with your child. You are building a legacy that will last a lifetime.

YOU MAY WONDER...

WHAT DOES THIS CHILD NEED MOST?

LOVE

is the ONE

thing they

need most.

SOMEONE MAY HAVE TOLD YOU THAT YOU WOULD NEVER EXPERIENCE LOVE LIKE THIS.

And they were right, of course.

What they may not have told you is how hard it would be to "like" them sometimes.

Beckham spends more time IN time-out than OUT.

Kai is terrified of the automatic flush in public restrooms. He would rather hold it than use it.

Sarah likes to put things up her nose--marbles, blueberries and six-inch noodles.

Lucas freaks out if different foods touch on the plate.

Macy sucks on her stuffed animals every night while she sleeps.

Annie refuses to wear anything but dresses that spin. If they don't spin, they don't go on Annie.

Eli calls his parents by their first name. He's two.

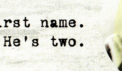

EVERY ONE OF THOSE KIDS HAS THE ADVANTAGE OF HAVING A PARENT WHO LOVES THEM REGARDLESS OF HOW . . . .

★ soon she takes her first steps.

★ fast he learns his ABCs.

★ quickly she potty trains.

★ hard he hits a Tee-ball.

★ well behaved they are in public.

With each marble or week that slips by, there are opportunities to demonstrate the one thing every child needs most.

How we love our kids while they are kids will impact them for the rest of their lives.

THIS DOESN'T NEED TO GET COMPLICATED. LOVE THEM FOR WHO THEY ARE AND THE WAY THEY ARE. WHEN YOU DO THIS, YOU WILL MAKE YOUR CHILD FEEL SIGNIFICANT AND GIVE THEM A SENSE OF SELF-WORTH.

Love them ... at their own pace.

"I've tried everything to get Jacob to go on the potty.
M and M's, the Elmo Potty DVD, even the "no diaper for the
weekend" trick. (i.e., the one invented by carpet cleaners)
And nothing worked. Finally, I gave up and let him take the
lead. And wouldn't you know it, a month later, he did it
all on his own."

Love them ... when they make mistakes.

"Whenever Corinne comes out of time-out (which is a LOT),
we make a point of hugging her and saying 'I love you.'
I like that it's a part of the ritual."

Love them ... regardless of performance.

"My son just started playing soccer, and he is not even
close to being the best player on the team. But every time
he's done, I tell him 'I love watching you play, buddy!'"

SO, BACK TO THE QUESTION:
WHAT DOES
YOUR CHILD
NEED MOST?

LOVE.

IF YOU DON'T GET THIS ONE RIGHT, THE REST REALLY DOESN'T MATTER

You can start proving to your child that you love them, the day they are born, with . . .

- ★ the words you say.
- ★ the people you invite into their lives.
- ★ the stories you tell them.
- ★ the games you play.

The time you spend this week showing your child you love them is the best way to play for keeps.

YOU MAY WONDER...

WILL MY LIFE EVER BE THE SAME AGAIN?

No, your life
will never be
the same.

SOME DAYS AS A PARENT, THINGS CHANGE SO FAST, AND NEW CHALLENGES COME SO QUICKLY, IT MAKES YOUR HEAD SPIN.

You spend six months convincing your child the pacifier is their best friend, only to find out its time to take it away so their teeth will come in straight. Just like the weather in Chicago, things just don't stay the same very long when you are a parent. If you don't like something, just wait five minutes and it will change.

Moments like these cause us to think back to our semi-carefree lives before the baby and wonder:

Will my _____ ever be the same again?

    body
    sleep
    sex
    dinner
    money
    living room
    vacations
    dinners
    phone conversations
    tv programs
    car
    refrigerator

WANT THE TRUTH?

1. YOU'LL CRY MORE.

It happens when you least expect it.

Seemingly innocent movies like <u>Toy Story 3</u> and <u>Up</u> will cause you to hide behind the bucket of popcorn to wipe the puddles of tears off your face before anyone catches you.

If you're not careful, certain songs like "Forever Young" and "Butterfly Kisses" will come on the radio and have you sobbing uncontrollably and swerving blindly down the road.

You'll cry when you miss them.
You'll cry when you're proud of them.
You'll cry when they put a dent in your brand new car.
You'll cry when they say, "I love you."
You'll cry when they drive you nuts.

The depth of love that you have for your child will surprise you emotionally and ambush your heart time after time.

2. YOU'LL LAUGH MORE.

(Sometimes you might laugh so hard you'll cry.)

2. YOU'LL LAUGH MORE.

Kids can be hilarious.

Kids can make parents sound hilarious.

Words you never thought you'd hear yourself say:

"Why is there a dirty diaper under my pillow?"
"Son, you have to go around the wall."
"You can't go to school naked."
"I feel so rested. I slept for three hours straight!"
"Sweety, why is your underwear thumb-tacked to the bed post?"
"I need to constantly wear a cup."
"Kids stop screaming, we're trying to have fun!"
"Don't tinkle in the potty when someone else is sitting on it."
"I have worn the same sweat pants for at least five days in a row!"
"It's okay, it's only cat food in his mouth."

_____ (add yours so you won't forget it)

Kids don't ever seem to run out of original material to keep you smiling. They can be incredibly entertaining if you are paying attention.

The amount of laughter that comes with having kids brings brand new joy and fulfillment into everyday life.

3. YOU'LL WORRY MORE.

Because you feel responsible . . .

* for providing their basic needs.
* for teaching them everything you know.
* for being emotionally available after a hard day.
* for making sure they turn out . . .(whatever that means).

The responsibility you feel may cause you to think surprisingly less about yourself and more about your child's future. As they grow, their successes become as important as your own.

SO, BACK TO THE QUESTION: WILL YOUR LIFE EVER BE THE SAME AGAIN? NOPE.

HAVING KIDS CHANGES YOU. AND THAT'S A GOOD THING. AND YOU AREN'T THE ONLY ONE. YOUR CHILD IS CHANGING TOO. EVERY DAY.

Your baby may be three months old today, but before you can blink, they will be six months . . . then nine months. Each stage only lasts a short time.

But whenever you look back through the days, weeks and months, you'll see how far they have come. You'll see the small investments you have made over time begin to pay off.

Shaping and raising a tiny human being is an incredible privilege. It is purposeful and significant—one of life's greatest gifts. Helping your child become the person they are meant to be makes all of the

crying,
laughing
and
worrying . . .

worth it.

It's worth it, because they are worth it.

YOU MAY WONDER...

WHO WILL THEY BECOME?

That's
still
a
mystery.

DEEP DOWN, WE ALL KNOW THAT ONE DAY 18 YEARS FROM NOW OUR KID WILL PACK THEIR BAGS AND WALK OUT THE FRONT DOOR.

Whether the thought depresses you, motivates you or makes you panic, your job as a parent is to prepare for that day.

YOU MIGHT THINK YOUR PRESCHOOLER HAS ASPIRATIONS TO BECOME:

a zookeeper in charge of rounding up stray animals.

an inventor of a new Olympic sport using a laundry basket, tricycle and a dog.

an airline pilot who still loves to make plane noises as they fly.

a doctor who cures the common cold and sadness at the same time.

a Pulitizer Prize winner whose work is all done in crayon on the walls.

REGARDLESS OF WHAT THEY ACCOMPLISH IN LIFE, IT'S IMPORTANT TO STAY FOCUSED ON WHAT REALLY MATTERS.

"Love the LORD your God with all your heart and with all your soul and with all your strength." Deuteronomy 6:5

A WISE AND TRUSTED LEADER, MOSES, ONCE TOLD A GROUP OF PARENTS, AUNTS, UNCLES, SINGLES, AND GRANDPARENTS THAT THE MOST IMPORTANT THING TO PASS ON TO EVERY CHILD IS A RELATIONSHIP WITH GOD. HE WANTED THEM TO SHOW THEIR CHILDREN HOW TO LOVE GOD WITH ALL THEIR HEARTS.

Why? Because the God who made your child and loves them most also knows what is best for them. He wants to take every child on a grand faith adventure that will capture their imagination for a lifetime. He plans to give their life purpose and fulfillment so they can truly live.

Who wouldn't want that for their child? As a parent, you have the greatest influence when it comes to shaping faith in your child.

And you can start now. It's never too early.

I know what you're thinking: "I haven't even had time for a shower, how can I do that?"

IT'S NOT AS HARD AS YOU MIGHT THINK. MOSES ADVISED PARENTS TO SIMPLY MAKE FAITH PART OF THEIR EVERYDAY LIVES. THERE'S NO BETTER WAY TO TALK ABOUT FAITH THAN TO INCORPORATE IT INTO WHAT YOU'RE ALREADY DOING EACH WEEK.

HERE ARE SOME SUGGESTIONS:

 BATH TIME: While they are splashing around in the tub, remind them that God made them just the way they are. Point out how incredible their eyes, ears, arms and feet are. Talk about all they can do because of the body God gave them.

 CUDDLE TIME: When you are tucking them in, or while they are calm and cuddly, sing a song or read a short and simple Bible story. Pray out loud, thanking God for loving them for who they are.

 DRIVE TIME: While you're in your car, listen to fun songs about God. Talk about how God does big things and loves to help each of us do big things, too.

 PLAY TIME: When they are playing, get down on their level and use their toys to act out a short scene from a simple Bible story, or explain how God wants them to share. Or take a walk and make a game of pointing out all the things that God has made.

When you use the rhythm of your routine each week to talk about God with your child, you allow their faith to develop naturally over the years.

SO, BACK TO THE QUESTION:
WHO WILL
THEY BECOME?

IT'S A MYSTERY.

BUT THE BEST PERSON TO INFLUENCE THEIR FUTURE IS YOU.

As a parent . . .

You have the most influence.
You have the most time with them.
You show them how you live your
faith out each week.

The Church exists to help build the faith of the next generation.
There are other adults who can support you because they've been
where you are now. There are other leaders who can influence your
child because they will show up consistently in their world week
after week. When you combine your influence, together you have
a far greater impact than any could have alone.

YOU HAVE 936 WEEKS TO GIVE YOUR CHILD THE FOUNDATION THEY WILL BUILD ON FOR THE REST OF THEIR LIVES. WHEN YOU FAST-FORWARD THROUGH THE WEEKS AND YEARS,

WHO DO YOU SEE?

Someone who loves God
Someone who loves others
Someone who really lives

SO START RIGHT NOW:

★ Prioritize your relationship with them.

★ Be present and dependable.

★ Love them regardless.

★ Welcome the changes.

★ Help them shape their faith.

PARENTING IS . . .

- ★ Full of messiness.
- ★ Full of beauty.
- ★ Full of patience.
- ★ Full of pain.
- ★ Full of changes.
- ★ Full of laughter.
- ★ Full of tears.
- ★ Full of love.
- ★ Full of God.
- ★ Full of wonder.

REALLY, ISN'T PARENTING WONDER-FULL?

authors

sue

When Sue Miller was a little, she wanted to be an actor. She used to act out plays in the basement with her stuffed animals. Today, she is an author, leader and gifted communicator with a passion to help good parents become great parents. She served as children's ministry director for 17 years at Willow Creek Community Church in Barrington, Ill., where she grew Promiseland into a cutting-edge children's ministry known around the world and wrote Making Your Children's Ministry the Best Hour of Every Kid's Week. In 2005, Sue moved her family to Atlanta and is now working for Orange and helping church leaders partner with parents.

holly

Holly Delich grew up in Chicago, Ill. As a child, she wanted to be a zookeeper but followed her mom (Sue Miller) around at Willow Creek Community Church and eventually became a full-time staffer in 1997, writing curriculum for their children's ministry. Since 2006, Holly has served at NorthPoint Community Church in Atlanta, Ga. as creative director of KidStuf. Her passion is to create experiences for families that inspire parents to apply God's big ideas with their kids at home where it really counts. She now has two sons of her own, Levi and Landon, who have inspired their mommy and grandma to write this book.

notes, thoughts & doodles